Wheels Make It Work

Natalie Scott

REAL LIFE readers™

Rosen Classroom™

New York

Wheels are round.
Wheels can roll.
Wheels can make things go.

Some machines need wheels to work.

A wheelbarrow has one wheel.
A wheelbarrow needs a wheel
to work.

A bike has two wheels.
A bike needs wheels
to work.

A tricycle has three wheels.
A tricycle needs wheels
to work.

A wheelchair has four wheels.
A wheelchair needs wheels
to work.

A car has four wheels.
A car needs wheels
to work.

This truck has eighteen wheels!
A truck needs wheels
to work.

Many machines need wheels
to work.
How many can you name?

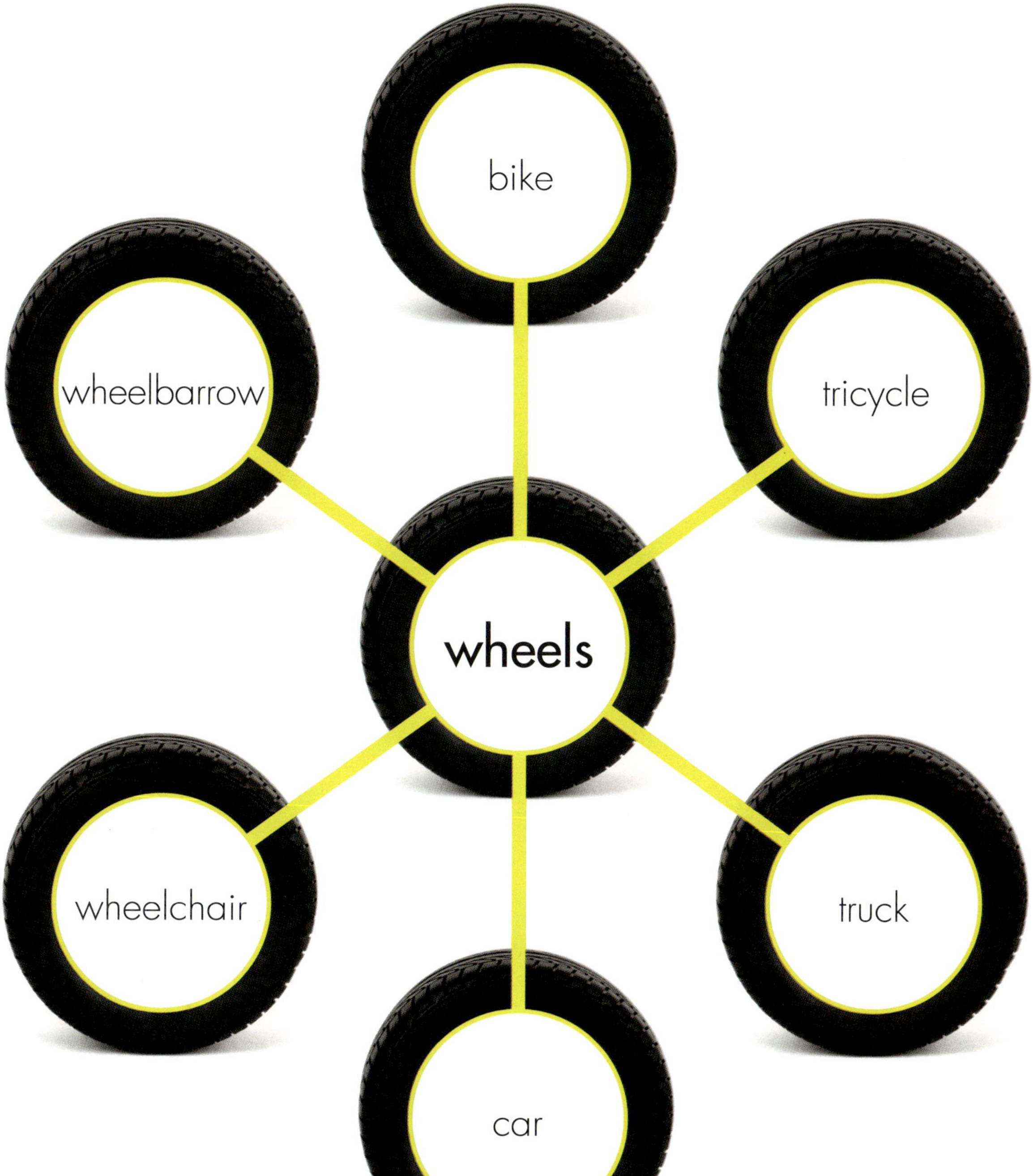
wheels
bike
tricycle
truck
car
wheelchair
wheelbarrow

Words to Know

bike

car

tricycle

truck

wheelbarrow

wheelchair